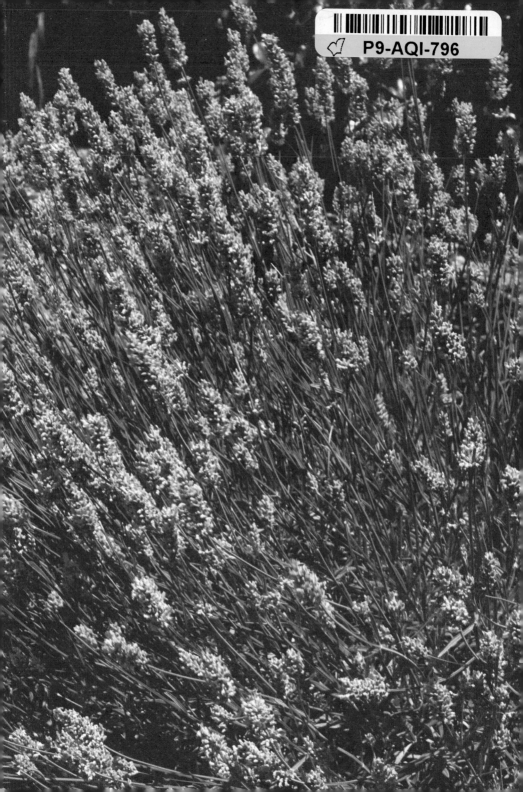

Gardening WITH THE EXPERTS

PERENNIALS

Gardening WITH THE EXPERTS

PERENNIALS

HUGH REDGROVE

HARLAXTON
PUBLISHING

Published by Harlaxton Publishing Ltd
2 Avenue Road, Grantham, Lincolnshire, NG31 6TA, United Kingdom.
A Member of the Weldon International Group of Companies.

First published in 1992.
Reprinted 1993

Publishing Manager: Robin Burgess
Project Coordinator: Mary Moody
Editor: Christine Mackinnon
Illustrator: Kathie Baxter Smith
Designed & produced for the publisher by Phillip Mathews Publishers
Produced in Singapore by Imago

British Library Cataloguing-in-Publication data.
A catalogue record for this book is available from the British Library.
Title: Gardening with the Experts: Perennials.
ISBN:1 85837 032 9

CONTENTS

INTRODUCTION

A perennial plant is one that can be expected to reappear every spring, will grow and flower during the summer year after year, then die down in winter. A hardy plant is one that will withstand the winter cold and damp. Naturally this hardiness will vary according to regional climate. Some hardy perennials lose all foliage in winter but others retain it in whole or in part.

Edged by timber logs, a cottage garden of mixed perennials.

*Tall stems of **lupins** as background accent plants.*

GARDEN BEDS

Beds or borders

In days gone by, perennial plants were usually grown in long straight beds known as herbaceous borders. This formal arrangement invariably used a hedge or a wall or possibly flowering shrubs as background — and naturally the taller varieties of plants were grouped at the back with shorter ones in front.

In recent years, however, Alan Bloom, a leading grower of hardy perennials in Britain, has been promoting the idea of island beds of informal shape, which has much to recommend it. Normally grass will surround such beds but when appropriate a pathway, curved where possible, can be used on one side. Many of the lower growing perennials look very attractive if allowed to spill over the edge when in full growth.

Plants in perennial borders should be arranged according to height — taller species at the back.

An established perennial border demonstrating mixed colour scheming.

A classical perennial border

Mixed borders

Some people now talk about cottage borders and try to reproduce the very informal planting usually associated with country cottages in Britain.

To obtain a continuously good effect, annuals and biennials are included in the planting and often a few shrubs, and possibly herbs. Such planting usually involves replanting the annuals much more frequently, but the result can be very charming and pleasurable.

Island beds

One advantage of the island bed is that it is usually sited well away from trees, with the result that the plants are sturdier and require less staking than in a border next to a hedge or wall. In selecting the plants for an island bed, the height of the tallest should not exceed half the total width of the border.

The taller plants are arranged in the centre, the shorter ones in front of them with the shortest of all near the verge. If it is possible to lay paving along the verge, set it so that the slabs are level with the lawn, facilitating mowing and eliminating edge trimming. The paving will allow the front row of plants to spill over the edge in a very attractive manner.

Opposite: Carefully consider colour scheming when arranging the border, ensuring flowers either contrast or complement each other.
Overleaf: Take advantage of a damp location to create a bog garden planted with moisture-loving perennials.

PREPARATION

Weeds

When preparing the site for a new bed or border it is important to eliminate perennial weeds. Docks, couch grass, bindweed, creeping thistle are all impossible to eradicate from a mixed perennial border, therefore they must be eliminated first.

This could take some months but with the aid of an all–purpose herbicide it is not impossible. (Weedkillers for driveways are not suitable.) Annual weeds such as groundsel, chickweed or shepherd's purse matter much less as these are more easily controlled by hoeing or mulching.

A mulch layer between plants will suppress weed growth.

Drainage and soils

Some gardeners will have the good fortune to have gardens of light alluvial soil or perhaps volcanic soils, others will have sandy or gravelly soils, while many others will have heavy loam or clay.

In the last category it will be necessary to ensure the border drains freely in times of heavy rain otherwise some plants may not thrive. If the ground is on a slope it should not be too difficult to shed rainwater but on a level site it is more difficult and drainage tiles may be needed.

One cannot expect all plants to flourish in wet and sticky soils over winter, especially as these soils, in some regions, may tend to bake hard in summer sun. Although there are a few that will grow in wet soils, a bog garden is the place to grow them.

The sandy, gravelly or volcanic soils are invariably free–draining and likely to dry out in summer. They will respond to dressings of peat, compost and manure. There are a few perennials such as *lupins* that do not thrive on alkaline soils and a test of the soil will indicate which species to avoid planting, if any.

A neutral soil with a reading of pH6 is an ideal; if the figure is much lower then an application of lime is recommended, after digging but before planting.

The site should be cultivated to a depth

***Limonium latifolium** is a perennial form, valued for its lilac flowers.*

of 30cm (1ft), wherever this can be done without bringing up subsoil or clay, at the same time adding compost and manure. To lighten heavy clay soil any organic material such as spent hops, seaweed, shredded garden rubbish, poultry or animal manure, peat and sand can all be worked in. A rotary hoe will do this admirably but often does not go deep enough to take the place of an initial digging.

Compost can be made in bins, a tumbler or directly on the ground.

15

PLANNING AND COLOUR

Planning

Undoubtedly the best results are obtained by planning the planting on graph paper (scale 1 cm to 1 metre [1/2 in to 3ft]) so that an assessment of the number of plants required and careful placement of them can be made.

An average density for planting is 4-5 plants per square metre (or square yard), but this will vary between the small plants at the front and the larger ones further back. In choosing the plants, personal likes and dislikes must be a first consideration; length of flowering season is important in order to get maximum effect; time of flowering should also be considered so as to avoid periods without flowers; heights also are very important. So, for the inexperienced, a good reference book is essential.

Paeony Jan van Laewen

The spire-like growth of delphiniums, verbascums, hollyhocks and the taller lilies should be intermingled with plants of a bushier nature; it is necessary also to place groups of late flowering plants in front of early flowering plants such as *watsonias, iris, campanulas* and spring bulbs so that the gaps left after flowering are not too obvious. It is also possible to plan for effect at a particular time of the year to avoid, say, mid-summer if that is the time you are normally away on holiday.

Colour

With all these factors to consider, the most important is apt to be forgotten — and that is colour.

As you plan, you can put together colour groupings which you have observed with pleasure elsewhere, and also avoid placing groups of the same colour and same flowering time close together, or others that you know will clash.

If you have duly attended to all the other factors, the result will be a pleasing and harmonious picture, for nature does not often clash her colours.

A great many books are available on perennials written by gardeners for the northern hemisphere and in the main this information is an excellent guide for cool regions. Be aware of seasonal and calendar

Vivid yellows and oranges combine colourfully.

variations. In warm regions where frosts are light or non-existent there are a number of perennials that will have great difficulty to flower satisfactorily.

This is not always appreciated by gardeners who have had their training in cold conditions. Peonies are a notable example, that despite an occasional exception seldom produces flowers in frost-free areas.

Other plants that may prove difficult are *Aconitum, Helleborus niger, Incarvillea, Linum perenne*, lupins, oriental poppy, *Primula florindae* (*Primula helodoxa* and

most others are quite good), *scabiosa, veronica, meconopsis, Trollius eruopaeus* (*Trollius ledebouri*, however, flowers well).

There may be exceptions to this list, but in most warmer regions these species are unlikely to be successful.

In warmer areas one has the opportunity grow many other plants of which very few have hardy or half hardy varieties, including: *Asclepias, Bletilla* orchids, Marguerite daisies, *Clivia, Dietes, Euchomis, Gloriosa, Hippeastrum, Isoplexis, Ageratum houstanum, Vallota, Veltheimia, Euryops, Impatiens, Canna.*

Overleaf: A lush waterside planting, showing variety in foliage colour and texture.

SPACING AND
MIXED BORDERS

Spacing

Generally it is best to plant groups of three or more plants of each variety although there are some which divide very easily, such as *Lobelia* 'Queen Victoria', that can be planted in groups of 5 to 10 quite close together. In many cases, if one is prepared to wait a year or two while temporarily using annuals and biennials to fill gaps, the stronger plants can be divided (see notes on propagation) in order to gradually fill the border fully.

In other cases division is not possible, for example, *Gypsophila, Limoniums* (statice), *Thalictrums* and *Eryngiums*. A few may be divided and replanted after growing for one full season, for example, Michaelmas (Easter) daisies (Aster) and *Helianthus* (sunflowers).

Mixed borders

In many cases gardeners prefer to use perennials in association with flowering shrubs and perhaps bulbs, in particular with camellias. While the ever-popular cultivars of *Camellia japonica* grow best in partial shade, a large proportion of perennials grow best in full sun.

In this situation you must choose perennials that are shade tolerant. On the other hand, cultivars of *Camellia reticulata* and their hybrids, together with all

Camellia sasanqua cultivars and most other hybrids such as 'Donation' or 'Spring Festival', grow well in full sun and are very suitable companions for perennials. There are, of course, a large number of other flowering shrubs that enjoy the sun. The choice of shrubs to use with perennials will be influenced by their colour, height and time of flowering.

It may be wise to remember that you may not get it right first time, but most perennial plants can be moved quite safely in winter or early spring, so experiment and improve arrangements with experience.

Mix perennials in beds with shrubs, annuals and perennials.

Opposite: A successful border should include perennials, bulbs and annuals.

A well-tended garden border, in the cottage style.

MAINTENANCE

Although less staking is required for borders in full sun that are away from trees, many gardens may be exposed to wind, so staking will be necessary. It can be very aggravating to admire a group of plants one day, only to find that they are almost flat the next day. Try as you might, it is then often impossible to tie them so that they look natural in manner.

Prevention is so much better than cure. The wise gardener will have a supply of small stakes in a convenient corner to put around the clumps in good time — before they fall over.

Twist ties and sometimes string will be needed. Prunings from many trees and shrubs are often suitable, particularly those from bamboo, apple trees or some conifers.

If evergreen, the prunings can be stowed away while the foliage dies off. For tall *gladioli, eucomis* and *delphiniums* a straight stake plus a twist tie is all that is required, the stem will require one each.

Another method is to stretch large mesh netting at a suitable height above the clump and allow stems to grow through it.

Early in the season before growth is much developed, weeds can be controlled safely by spraying with a weedicide, so long as the spray nozzle is kept close to the soil on a still day.

Later, hoeing may be necessary and very likely some hand weeding. An annual dressing of fertiliser will encourage most plants to flower more freely, and a general purpose fertiliser (5% N : 5% P : 5% K) is

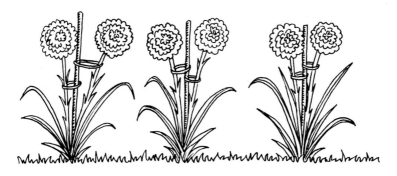

*Tall-growing perennials such as **dahlias** and **chrysanthemums** require staking.*
*Opposite: **Iris kaempferi** 'Summer storm' has deep purple petals.*

Liquid fertiliser applied with a watering can.

quite suitable and should be applied early in the spring.

Poultry manure is often available and it makes an excellent low cost spring mulch when applied at a depth of not more than 3cm (1.5in).

Summer maintenance should include removal of spent flowerheads, watering during dry spells, and mulching with any fine organic material in order to prevent the moisture from drying up rapidly.

In autumn or early winter most of the top growth should be cut down and composted. Some summer flowering plants have evergreen foliage and this should be trimmed, for example, *Kniphofia* (redhot pokers), some day-lilies, *Aristia* and *Dietes*.

DAHLIAS AND CHRYSANTHEMUMS

If these plants are included in the border they will add materially to the display in late summer and autumn.

The modern *dahlia* flowers very freely and is available in many shapes and sizes. Of *chrysanthemums*, the late flowering 'Korean' *chrysanthemums* are probably the easiest for the non-specialist and may be had in single and double forms and a variety of colours. Seed strains are offered and produce a mixed bag. Probably half should be discarded with the best grown on for the future.

The great advantage of the 'Koreans' is their hardiness through the winter and they require a minimum of spraying to keep them healthy. Neither is it necessary to disbud them, although some 'stopping' may be required early in the season.

Mulch well for good results.

Trimming back summer growth.

Dahlias.

PERENNIAL FAVOURITES

The following are some favourite plants that everyone likes to grow.
OO = maximum sun all day; O = sun; w = part shade; l = full shade.

NAME	HEIGHT	SUN/ SHADE	COLOUR	FLOWERING TIME	REMARKS
Alchemilla mollis (Lady's Mantle)	30 cm (12 in)	Ow	yellow	spring	attractive foliage
Anchusa (Morning Glory)	1 m+ (3 ft+)	O	brilliant blue	spring	short-lived
Anemone japonica (Windflower)	70 cm (28 in)	Ow	white, pink	autumn	
Aquilegia vulgaris 'McKana' Hybrids	90 cm (35 in)	Ow	various	spring	long spurs
Aster (Michaelmas daisy)	60 cm- 1 m (2-3 ft)		white, pink, red, blue to name	summer	very bushy
Campanula latifolia (Bellflower)	30 cm- 1 m (1-3 ft)	Ow Ow	lilac blue white, blue, violet	spring spring	
Coreopsis grandifolia	60 cm (2 ft)	O	yellow	late spring	single or double
Delphinium elatum 'Pacific' Hybrids	1.5 m (4 ft 6 in)	O	all shades blue& white	summer	beware slugs
Dianthus (pinks, carnations)	10-50 cm (4-20 in)	O	all colours, very varied	spring	they like lime
Erigeron (Fleabane)	60 cm (2 ft)	O	mauve, pink or violet blue	spring	
Gaillardia (Blanket flower)	60 cm (2 ft)	O	yellow & red–yellow	summer	

NAME	HEIGHT	SUN/ SHADE	COLOUR	FLOWERING TIME	REMARKS
Helenium (Coneflower)	60 cm- 1 m (2-3 ft)	O	yellow to red-brown	spring/ summer	
Hosta (Plantain lily)	30-90 cm (1-3 ft)	w	mauve	spring/ summer	mainly for attractive foliage
Hemerocallis (Day lily)	90 cm- 1.2 m (3-4 ft)	Ow	pink, maroon, yellow, orange	spring/ summer	
Kniphofia (Redhot Poker)	1-2 m (3-6 ft)	Ow	scarlet, orange, yellow cultivars	all year	
Lupinus polyphyllus (Lupins)	60 cm- 1.2 m (2-4 ft)	O	all colours	spring	cool regions only
Nepeta faassenii (catmint)	30 cm (1 ft)	Ow	mauve	spring/ summer	
Paeonia (Peony)	80 cm- 1 m (2-3 ft)	O	white, pink, red	spring	cool regions only
Phlox	60 cm- 1 m (2-3 ft)	Ow	white, crimson pink, scarlet	summer	not clay soils
Pyrethrum	60-90 cm (2-3 ft)	O	white, pink, red	spring	not clay soils
Rudbeckia (Coneflower)	60 cm- 1.2 m (2-3 ft)	O	yellow	summer	single or double
Salvia x *superba*	75 cm (20 in)	Ow	violet purple	spring/ summer	
Verbascum (Mullein)	1-1.5 m (3-5 ft)	O	yellow, white, also coppery	spring/ summer	some are biennial

Geranium 'Alcherilla mollis'.

Perennials for wet places

The following are some perennials which require wetter than average conditions. Gardeners lucky enough to be able to provide them will be able to grow many beautiful plants that are rarely seen. Modern water irrigation systems will help in borderline cases.

OO = maximum sun all day; O = sun; w = part shade; l = full shade.

NAME	HEIGHT	SUN/ SHADE	COLOUR	FLOWERING TIME	REMARKS
Astilbe hybrids	60 cm (2 ft)	Ow	white, pink, red	spring	
Astilbe simplicifolia	1.2 m (4 ft)	Ow	pink spikes	summer	
Aruncus sylvester (Goats beard)	1.75 m (5 ft)	wl	creamy white plumes	summer	
Candelabra primulas *Primula helodoxa*	75 cm (30 in)	w	yellow tiers	spring	sheltered
Primula florindae, *Primula pulverulenta*, *Primula aurantiaca*	60 cm (2 ft)	w	yellow, orange, crimson	spring	sheltered
Filipendula rubra venusta	2 m (6 ft)	Ow	feathery pink	summer	foliage good
Gunnera manicata	2 m (6ft)	w		spring/ summer	
Hakonecloa macra 'Aureola'	25 cm (10 in)	Ow	yellow foliage	winter/ spring	a grass
Hosta - all species and cultivars	30 cm- 1.2 m (1-4 ft)	wl	green or variegated foliage	spring	flowers mauve

PERENNIAL FAVOURITES

NAME	HEIGHT	SUN/SHADE	COLOUR	FLOWERING TIME	REMARKS
Iris laevigata	1 m (3ft)	Ow	various	spring	
Iris kaempferi	1.5 m (4 ft 6 in)	Ow	white, blue, lilac, violet	spring/ summer to 20 cm diam.	open flat flowers
Lobelia fulgens 'Flamingo'	1 m (3 ft)	w	pink flower spikes	late summer	new
'Queen Victoria'	80 cm (32 in)	w	scarlet flower spikes	summer	
Lobelia syphilitica	80 cm (32 in)	Ow	blue flower spikes	summer	
Lobelia verdrariense	1 m (3 ft)	Ow	rich purple	late summer	
Lythrum salicaria	1.5 m (4 ft 6 in)	O	rosy purple spikes	summer	vigorous
Mimulus lutea (Monkey musk)	50 cm (20 in)	Ow	yellow, bronze, red	spring/ summer	spreading
Onoclea sensibilis	50 cm (20 in)	l	spreading fern	spring	deciduous
Osmunda regalis (Royal fern)	2 m (6 ft)	w	very large fronds		deciduous
Rodgersia pinnata 'Superba'	1 m (3 ft)	w	pink spikes	summer	
Trollius europaeus (Globe flower)	50 cm (20 in)	O	yellow globular	spring	cool only
Trollius ledebouri	50 cm (20 in)	O	golden yellow	spring	most regions

Plants for shade

There are considerable differences in the degree of shade required—in cool regions, some of these plants will almost prefer full sun, —the same plants in hotter regions will prefer some degree of shade.

A few plants indicated thus * will always prefer to be grown in the shade of trees, especially in the warmer sunny areas. Areas under trees may become very dry due to tree roots, so an annual mulch of compost or poultry manure will often work wonders.

Alstromeria pulchella	Impatiens
Aquilegia	Iris foetidissima *
Acanthus *	Liriope muscari *
Arthropodium cirrhatum	Meconopsis
Anemone japonica	Mertensia
Bergenia	Myosotidum *
Billbergia	Omphalodes
Campanula persicifolia	Pachysandra
Campanula latifolia	Polygonatum *
Clivia miniata *	Polyanthus
Convallaria * (Lily of the Valley)	Primula
Dicentra	Platycodon
Digitalis	Rodgersia
Epimedium	Solidago
Gunnera	Thalictrum
Helleborus *	Trillium *
Hemerocallis	Tradescantia
Heuchera	

Perennials that need frequent division

The following give their best results if divided and replanted every second or third season:

Aster novi–belgii	Helianthus
Aster novae–angliae	Lychnis viscaria
Anthemis	Monarda
Artemisia lactiflora	Oenothera fruticosa
Dianthus	Physostegia
Erigeron	Rudbeckia
Gaillardia	Sidalcea
Helenium	Solidago

Rich soil in necessary for intensive gardening.

PERENNIAL PROPAGATION

Seed propagation

A number of species are still grown from seed since species reproduce true from seed so long as there is no opportunity for cross–fertilisation. However, selections with improved characteristics called cultivars are numerous and must be increased by vegetative means. In some cases seedsmen have 'fixed' a number of strains by line breeding as these breed true, or nearly so. These include cultivars of *aquilegia, althaea rosea* (hollyhocks), *geum* and *delphinium*.

Seed should not be used when named cultivars are superior. To illustrate this

Plants with small roots are easily propagated by division.

point take a look at *aquilegias*. 'McKana' long-spurred hybrids are a lovely mixture of bright colours with large flowers and long spurs. None of the individual colours would breed true. But there are several named cultivars which do—'Crimson Star' (crimson and white) and 'Nora Barlow' (double pink and green). But for other colours it is necessary to go back to the species, for example *aquilegia caerulea* (60cm [24in] with blue and white flowers) and *aquilegia longissima* (70cm [28in] with glaucous leaves and 15cm [6in] spurs on the yellow flowers).

The single pyrethrum *chrysanthemum coccineum* is another example. Seed strains of pink and red come sufficiently true to have superseded the old cultivars 'E.M. Robinson' and 'Harold Robinson'. But the named doubles must be grown from divisions. This plant, as well as the cultivars of *scabiosa caucasica* should not be divided until growth has begun in spring. For these plants division in autumn especially in cool climates can be fatal.

Division

There are many cultivars of perennial plants which may be increased from the division of the rootstock quite easily, such as *aster novi-belgii, helianthus, helenium, monarda, physostegia*, to suggest just a few.

This is normally done in late winter to

early spring, by which time many of the new growths will have begun a new root system, so that they may be replanted outdoors or potted straight away. In all cases, when more increase is required top cuttings may be taken when the shoots have reached 20cm (8in); these cuttings are then rooted under glass.

There are some vigorous perennials which develop into large clumps requiring considerable physical effort to break them up. One can be faced with a solid clump of interlocking roots, say 30cm (12in) across. Two border forks driven back to back and close together into the clump is often the only way to make an impression. *Hosta, hemerocallis, astilbe* are examples. In the case of *hostas* and others it is also necessary to use a strong knife, cutting the crown vertically to separate the growth buds each with its share of the root system. Each strong bud will develop into a satisfactory plant in the first season. But the full beauty of foliage and flower will not develop until

Agapanthus 'Blue Nile'.

the second or third season.

Alstroemeria, on the other hand, should be divided and replanted when they are dormant at the end of summer. Even the cultivar 'Walter Fleming' can be safely handled then and will make new growth before the winter.

Paeonia officinalis, paeonia lactiflora and *paeonia lobata*, which are hardy, tough plants, should be divided in autumn by cutting the roots with a sharp knife to leave one, two, or three eyes on each plant. They may be replanted straight away. Delay after autumn means less growth and fewer, if any, flowers. Once planted, leave undisturbed for up to 10 years.

Propagation from cuttings

Perennials which form a woody rootstock are normally propagated from cuttings first

Divide matted plants using two garden forks, back to back.

taken in spring from the first flush of growth and subsequently as further suitable growths develop. The cuttings are struck in sand under close conditions with or without bottom heat after the application of hormone powder suitable for soft wood. *Lythrum, anthemis, gaura, scrophularia, aster amellus, gypsophila* 'Rosy Veil' are examples, while the more popular *gypsophila* 'Flamingo' and *gypsophila* 'Bristol Fairy' need ideal conditions for rooting or else they must be grafted.

Named cultivars of *lupinus polyphyllus* and *delphinium elatum* need special treatment. The roots should be lifted in early winter from open ground and planted in a cold frame or a sheltered indoor site in warm regions. As growth develops the cuttings are removed when 7cm (2 1/2in) long and with a solid heel. Often a second and possibly a third batch may be taken, after which the stock plants are discarded. Both these plants must be rooted in cool conditions with little or no artificial heat

Cuttings should be taken during early spring or autumn.

and shaded if the sun is strong. Hormones will assist rooting.

Campanula persicifolia and some other *campanulas* make numerous small white shoots around the crowns of one year old plants. Lift the plants about mid-winter and use these small shoots, with or without green leaves, as cuttings from 1.5 cm to 2.5 cm (1/2in to 1in)long. Dibble them into sandboxes 2.5cm (1in) apart with the tips at ground level. Usually all will root and if planted out later in light soil will make good clumps by autumn.

Grafting gypsophilas

The two aforementioned *gypsophilas* are often grafted to obtain a better 'take' than when grown from cuttings. Sow seed of *gypsophila paniculata* in early spring and plant out in early summer to produce a batch of rootstocks. These are lifted in the winter with the root systems complete and bedded outdoors if necessary.

Roots of pencil thickness are cut up into 7cm (2 1/2in lengths with the tops cut square, and giving the bases a sloping cut. When your stock plants of *gypsophila* 'Bristol Fairy' and 'Flamingo' have begun growth these sections of root are cleft in the centre and a wedge-shaped scion of the desired cultivar is inserted, with the cambium layers lined up on one side. The scion may be held in position in any way convenient but good results are obtained with no binding at all. The grafted roots are dibbled into sand in boxes or tubes and kept in close conditions. The advantage of boxes or tubes is that the plants are more easily hardened off.

Root cuttings

A number of perennials may be propagated by means of root cuttings, which is a

The fluffy mauve-blue flowers of **Ageratum**.

Remove any woody chutes or dead roots with secateurs.

convenient method. The stock plants should be grown in the open ground rather than in planter bags because the thick cuttings root and shoot much better than thin cuttings. Generally they need to be pencil thickness or thicker except in cases where plants normally have thin roots.

The following are usually grown from root cuttings: *papaver orientale, verbascums, romneya coulteri, anchusa italica* and *catananche caerulea*.

The following have thinner roots but the same principles apply: *primula denticulata, anemone japonica, phlox paniculata. Phlox* plants produced in this way are normally free from eelworm, which is a serious disease in some countries.

There are some tuberous plants that

Lupinus polyphyllus (*Russell hybrid*).

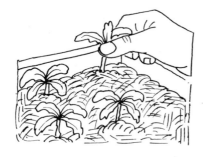

Tip cuttings should be placed in moist compost.

Mist propagation

Generally speaking, only a few herbaceous perennials get any benefit from mist propagation and in the cases of *pelargoniums* (all types) and silver-leaved plants mist is positively harmful and would lead to a lot of stem rot.

Pelargonium (Regal) stock plants should be cut back in late-summer while the weather is warm and growth is active.

The new growth will provide excellent cuttings for rooting in frames or a cool greenhouse and may be grown on for a good display the following spring and onwards.

have numerous dormant eyes, such as tuberous *iris, acorus calamus, zantedeschia* and *liatris spicata*. It is possible to propagate these by removing the eyes with part of the tuber, treating them with fungicide and striking them in a sterilised medium. With *zantedeschia* the fungicide treatment is especially important as the corms rot easily after damage. The tubers should be in a dormant state at the time of treatment.

Foliage cuttings

Lachenalia pearsonii may be increased by cutting the mature foliage horizontally into strips 8cm (3in) wide, treating with hormones and setting the sections into sandboxes (lower edge in the sand) in a cool greenhouse. Numerous small bulbs will form on this edge and in due course may be separately boxed. *Haemanthus katherinae* (Blood lily) may be propagated in the same manner, inserting the leaf cuttings in sand in mid-summer.

Insert leaf cuttings in moist sand.

Opposite: **Iris Louisiana** *'Liptight'*

PESTS AND DISEASES

Young succulent growth in the spring will often attract slugs and snails. Snail pellets are usually an effective remedy and easy to apply.

Hostas and some *campanulas* are often damaged by pests and it is especially necessary to watch the *hostas* because they are grown mainly for their foliage, which can be perforated so easily. *Delphiniums* often fail when tiny slugs eat the embryo shoots during winter. To keep the slugs off put an 8cm (3in) mound of sharp sand or fine scoria over the whole crown when you cut away the old stems in autumn. The new shoots should then be quite strong when they emerge.

Aphids may be troublesome and spraying with any insecticide will control them, but a systemic material will give lasting control. Caterpillars are also best controlled with a systemic spray and they usually appear in summer.

Protect young plants from snails and slugs.

Opposite: **Chrysanthemum frutescens**.

INDEX